500+ SUPER INTERESTING HOCKEY FACTS FOR KIDS

WILD NICKNAMES, RECORD BREAKS AND HOCKEY'S GREATEST WONDERS!

Michelle Weiss

TABLE OF CONTENTS

Introduction 1

Hockey Firsts 2

And the Award Goes To… 11

The Coveted Cup 15

The Rulebook 23

Where's Stanley Now? 32

Impressive Numbers 39

The Women of Hockey 44

They're Called What? 49

Hockey's Greatest Records 56

Traditions and Superstitions 70

One for the Teams 73

Hockey History 78

Incredible Rookies 84

Notable Players 86

Going for Olympic Gold 92

Hockey Around the World 97

College Hockey 99

Fun Facts 101

INTRODUCTION

Ice hockey is the most popular winter team sport in the world, boasting millions of players across the globe. Whether it's with professional players breaking records in the National Hockey League (NHL), countries around the world competing for gold at the Olympics, or just young kids playing with their friends in the backyard, hockey is an inspiring sport to play and watch. Besides being the most popular winter team sport, it's also the most difficult. The many factors of the game—skating, scoring, fighting, and everything in between—create an exciting, fast-paced atmosphere that awes us time and again. Hockey inspires people worldwide to give their all in whatever they do, whether playing in a rink or going to school.

In this book, you'll uncover facts about the amazing sport of ice hockey. Not only is there information about NHL records, the inspiring feats of individual players, rules of the game, and women's hockey, but also an overview of hockey's long history, fun stories about where the Stanley Cup has traveled, hockey players' wacky nicknames, and much more. You'll discover some of the greatest hockey players ever to hit the ice and the most incredible things they've accomplished.

With over 500 facts to discover, you'll be well on your way to becoming a hockey expert by the time you've read them all. Even after you've read from cover to cover, you can come back time and again to remember some of the greatest moments in all of hockey history.

Whether you're a dedicated fan or a newcomer to the sport, this book will captivate and inspire you with fascinating facts about the ice hockey world.

HOCKEY FIRSTS

When records were established, legends
were created, and history was made

1. Marc Crawford, coach of the Colorado
   Avalanches, was the first rookie head coach to
   win the Jack Adams Award.

2. Bob Gainey of the Montreal Canadiens won the
   first Selke Trophy in 1978 and then again for
   the next three years.

3. In October 1957, Maurice "Rocket" Richard
   became the first NHL player to score 500
   goals in his career.

4. The United States won the first World Cup of
   Hockey, led by players including Brett Hull,
   Mike Richter, and John LeClair.

5. Stan Mikita is the first NHL player credited
   with curving the blade of his hockey stick.

6. Alexei Kovalev of the New York Rangers and Pittsburgh Penguins was the first Russian-born player to be drafted in the first round of the NHL draft.

7. Paul Coffey was the first defenseman to have two 40-goal seasons.

8. The Montreal Canadiens made history in 1920 when they beat the Quebec Bulldogs 16-3, becoming the first team in the NHL to score 16 goals in a game.

9. George Hainsworth was the first goaltender to record 20 or more shutouts in one season, achieving 22 shutouts in 44 games during the 1928-29 season.

10. Maurice Richard was the first NHL player to score 50 goals in a season.

11. Neal Broten was the first American-born NHL player to have 100 or more points in a season.

12. Clint Benedict was the first goaltender to wear a mask in an NHL game, as his nose had been broken in a previous game. However, he only wore it for a few games.

13. The first U.S. team to play in the Stanley Cup finals was the Portland Rosebuds. They played against the Montreal Canadiens in 1916.

14. Jack Marshall was the first hockey player in history to win the Stanley Cup with four teams: Winnipeg Victorias, Montreal AAA, Montreal Wanderers, and Toronto Blueshirts.

15. John Ross Roach was the first goaltender to become a captain. He played for the Toronto St. Patricks and became the captain for the 1924-25 season.

16. The first U.S. team to win the Stanley Cup was the Seattle Metropolitans.

17. Bernie Federko of the St. Louis Blues and Detroit Red Wings was the first NHL player to record 50 or more assists in 10 consecutive seasons.

18. The first player to win the Hart Memorial Trophy for the NHL MVP by unanimous vote was Wayne Gretzky in the 1981-82 season.

19. Bobby Hull was the first NHL player to record two 50-goal seasons in a row.

20. The first player to wear the number 99 jersey was Joe Lamb; it later became the number of the legendary Wayne Gretzky.

21. Vincent Damphousse was the first player in history to lead three different NHL teams in scoring. He played for the Montreal Canadiens, Toronto Maple Leafs, and Edmonton Oilers.

22. Billy Burch, born in New York, was the first native U.S. NHL player. He played forward for multiple NHL teams, including the Boston Bruins and Chicago Blackhawks.

23. The first goaltender to consistently wear a mask was Jacques Plante of the Montreal Canadiens in 1959. He wore homemade ones during practice but not during games until a shot clipped his head. He then insisted to his coach that he wouldn't return to the ice without one.

24. The Montreal Wanderers were the first to engrave their players' names on the Stanley Cup in 1907.

25. Dan Bain of the Winnipeg Victorias was the first pro hockey player to score the winning goal in overtime to win the Stanley Cup.

26. The 1988 Edmonton Oilers was the first team to pose for a picture with the Stanley Cup right after winning it.

27. Dit Clapper was the first hockey player inducted into the Hockey Hall of Fame before the standard three-year waiting period in 1947.

28. In 2000, Mario Lemieux was the first player in NHL history to play for a team he also owned when he returned to the ice with the Pittsburgh Penguins.

29. The Detroit Red Wings and Montreal Canadiens made hockey history when they became the first teams to play each other at the Stanley Cup Finals for three years, from 1954 to 1956. The Red Wings won the first two years, and the Canadiens took the third.

30. Irvine Bailey was the first NHL player to have his jersey retired. He made valuable contributions to the Toronto Maple Leafs team but suffered an injury that put him off the ice for good.

31. Marian Hossa became the first player to play in the Stanley Cup Finals three consecutive years on three different teams. He played for the Pittsburgh Penguins, Detroit Red Wings, and Chicago Blackhawks and only won the cup for the third time.

32. The Edmonton Oilers became the first NHL team in history to achieve 400 goals in a season, with Wayne Gretzky and Kari Jurri leading the offensive players. They later upped the record to 446.

33. Willie O'Ree was the first Black player in NHL history. He debuted with the Boston Bruins in 1958.

34. Nicklas Lidström, born in Sweden, was the first European player to win the Conn Smythe trophy. He was also the first European-born player to captain his team (the Detroit Red Wings) to a Stanley Cup win.

35. Fred Sasakamoose is credited as the first Indigenous person to play in the NHL. He made his debut with the Chicago Blackhawks in 1954. Some believe that there were earlier Indigenous players, but records are unclear.

36. Georges Vezina—the player for whom the Vezina Trophy is named—performed the first shutout in NHL history in 1918. The Montreal Canadiens beat the Toronto Maple Leafs 9-0.

37. Paul Thompson of the Chicago Blackhawks scored the first-ever NHL goal against a brother when he scored past his goaltender brother Cecil Thompson of the Boston Bruins in 1930.

38. On December 8, 1987, Ron Hextall of the Philadelphia Flyers became the first player to shoot the puck the entire length of the ice and into an open net.

39. On December 1, 1940, four sets of brothers appeared in the same game, two on each team, between the Chicago Blackhawks and New York Rangers.

40. Yutaka Fukufuji was the first Japanese hockey player to play in the NHL, playing as a goaltender for the Los Angeles Kings in 2007.

41. Patrick Roy of the Montreal Canadiens, Colorado Avalanches, and Dallas Stars was the first goaltender to win 500 games.

42. Hockey legend Wayne Gretzky was the first NHL player to score 50 goals in one season during the 1981-82 season. Only two other players have earned this achievement since then.

43. The Boston Bruins signed Bobby Orr in 1971 with the first million-dollar contract in NHL history.

44. Mario Lemieux was the first player in the NHL to score five goals in five ways in one game: full-strength, power play, short-handed, penalty shot, and open net.

45. The first goaltender to score a goal in an NHL game was Ron Hextall of the Philadelphia Flyers.

46. Gordie Howe was the first player to lead the NHL in scoring four seasons in a row.

47. Phil Esposito of the Boston Bruins became the first NHL player to achieve 100 points in a season in 1969.

AND THE AWARD GOES TO...

All about hockey's most prestigious individual awards.

48. The Professional Hockey Writers Association votes on the winners of most individual trophies.

49. The Hart Trophy was the NHL's first individual trophy. It was named after Dr. David Hart, whose son Cecil worked in the Montreal Canadiens' office.

50. The Hart Memorial Trophy is given to the league's most valuable player or MVP.

51. Every year, the NHL playoff MVP receives the Conn Smythe Trophy.

52. The Vezina Trophy is awarded each season to the NHL's best goaltender.

53. The William M. Jennings Trophy is given to the goaltender(s) who let in the fewest goals every season.

54. The Calder Memorial Trophy is awarded to the best rookie of the season.

55. The Calder Memorial Trophy was initially called the Rookie of the Year reward. Frank Calder bought a trophy every year for the winner, so the NHL established a permanent trophy in his honor.

56. The James Norris Memorial Trophy is awarded each season to the best defenseman.

57. Every season, the league's top scorer receives the Art Ross Trophy.

58. The Lady Byng Memorial Trophy is offered to the most sportsmanlike player with the best skill.

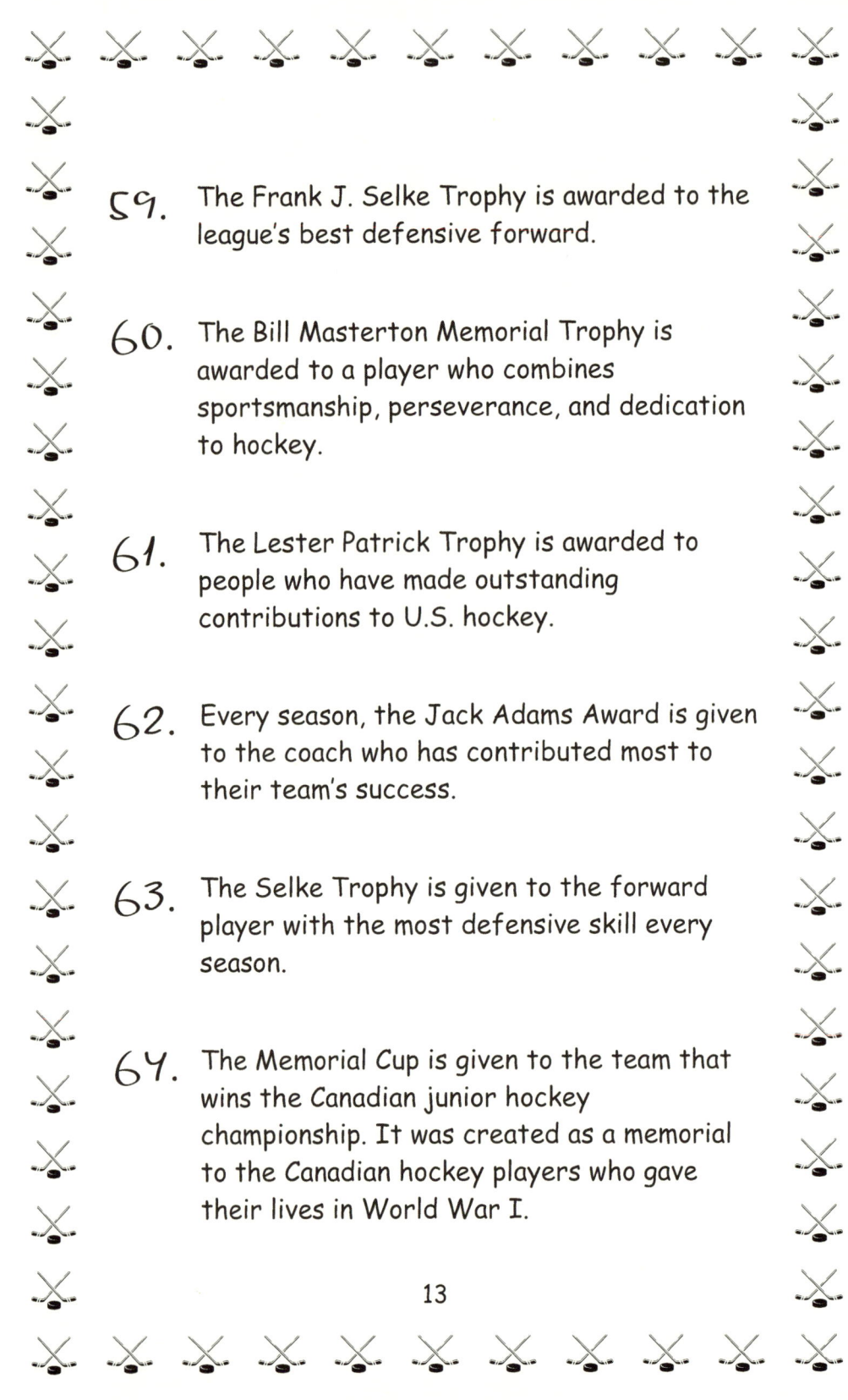

59. The Frank J. Selke Trophy is awarded to the league's best defensive forward.

60. The Bill Masterton Memorial Trophy is awarded to a player who combines sportsmanship, perseverance, and dedication to hockey.

61. The Lester Patrick Trophy is awarded to people who have made outstanding contributions to U.S. hockey.

62. Every season, the Jack Adams Award is given to the coach who has contributed most to their team's success.

63. The Selke Trophy is given to the forward player with the most defensive skill every season.

64. The Memorial Cup is given to the team that wins the Canadian junior hockey championship. It was created as a memorial to the Canadian hockey players who gave their lives in World War I.

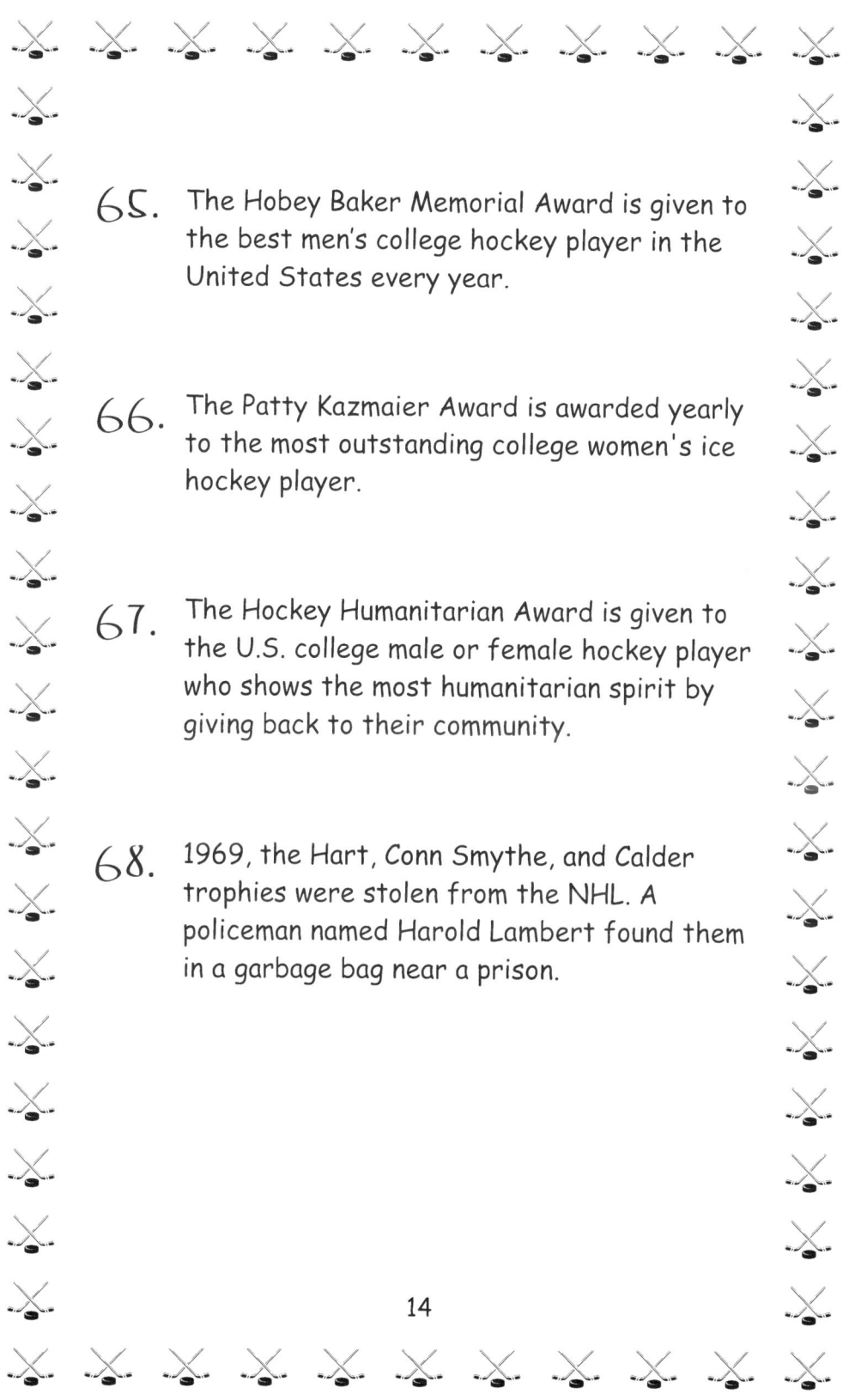

65. The Hobey Baker Memorial Award is given to the best men's college hockey player in the United States every year.

66. The Patty Kazmaier Award is awarded yearly to the most outstanding college women's ice hockey player.

67. The Hockey Humanitarian Award is given to the U.S. college male or female hockey player who shows the most humanitarian spirit by giving back to their community.

68. 1969, the Hart, Conn Smythe, and Calder trophies were stolen from the NHL. A policeman named Harold Lambert found them in a garbage bag near a prison.

THE COVETED CUP

Covering the playoffs, the finals, the champions, and the Stanley Cup.

69. The Stanley Cup is the oldest professional sports trophy.

70. Even though the Chicago Blackhawks had a 14-win, 25-loss, and nine-tie record with a .325 winning percentage in the 1937-38 season, they still won the Stanley Cup.

71. The Montreal Canadiens were the first NHL team to win five Stanley Cups from 1956 to 1960.

72. During the 1993 playoffs, 28 of the games went into overtime. Eventually, the Montreal Canadiens won the Stanley Cup, beating out the Los Angeles Kings.

73. The St. Louis Blues lost the Stanley Cup in a four-game sweep three consecutive years from 1968-1970.

74. Ray Bourque, a defenseman for the Boston Bruins and Colorado Avalanches, played 22 years for the NHL before winning his first Stanley Cup in his final season.

75. In 2003, LEGO built two replicas of the Stanley Cup out of 6000 LEGO bricks.

76. Every player on a team who wins the Stanley Cup gets a miniature Stanley Cup with their teammates' names engraved on it.

77. The Stanley Cup is engraved with the title "Dominion Hockey Challenge Cup," as Lord Stanley, who first bought and donated the cup, didn't want it to be named after him. However, the trustees in charge of the cup decided otherwise.

78. When a team wins the Stanley Cup, each player and team official gets to spend one day with it.

79. When the five bands of the Stanley Cup are all full, the top band (the oldest one) is retired to the Hockey Hall of Fame, and a new band is added to the bottom.

80. The first time a correction was made to a misspelled name on the Stanley Cup was in 1996 for Adam Deadmarsh, whose last name was engraved as "Deadmarch."

81. In 2010, Patrick Kane scored the winning goal to clinch the Stanley Cup for the Chicago Blackhawks for the first time in 49 years. He hit the puck into the goal, but there was immediate confusion as it seemed to have disappeared. It turned out the puck had gotten stuck underneath the net.

82. Phil Bourque is the only player to have his name engraved on the outside and inside of the Stanley Cup. He opened it when he heard a rattling noise and decided to engrave his name.

83. The names engraved on the Stanley Cup are stamped on. The process is so meticulous that stamping each name takes about a half hour.

84. The 1951 Stanley Cup finals between the Montreal Canadiens and Toronto Maple Leafs was the only time a playoff game series had every game go into overtime.

85. In 1962, a Montreal Canadiens fan tried to steal the Stanley Cup from the Chicago Blackhawks while it was on display.

86. The Stanley Cup bowl had to be replaced in 1970 because the original had become too fragile. The original bowl is on display at the Hockey Hall of Fame.

87. There are three Stanley Cups that exist today: the original bowl, the Presentation Cup that travels around throughout the year to hospitals, events, and players' homes, and a replica cup that is displayed at the Hockey Hall of Fame when the real cup is traveling.

88. The Stanley Cup Finals has only been decided in a seventh game overtime twice.

89. The Montreal Canadiens reached the Stanley Cup finals every year from 1951 to 1960 and won five championships from 1956 to 1960.

90. Each championship-winning team can engrave up to 52 names on the Stanley Cup when they win it.

91. In 1902, the Toronto Wellingtons and Winnipeg Victorias played for the Stanley Cup. In those days, it was hard to spread information quickly, so the president of the Ontario Hockey Association came up with a new way to announce the series' results to Toronto fans. If Toronto won, the train traveling through the city would blow its whistle twice. If they lost, it would blow the whistle three times. Unfortunately, Toronto fans heard the whistle blow three times.

92. During a Stanley Cup match between the Rat Portage Thistles and Ottawa Silver Seven in 1903, the weather was so warm that the puck fell through a hole in the ice.

93. In Game 4 of the 1988 Stanley Cup finals, the lights went out late in the second period due to a power failure. The game was stopped and rescheduled for two nights later.

94. Only four teams have returned from a three-game deficit in the Stanley Cup playoffs to win the series: the Toronto Maple Leafs in 1942, the New York Islanders in 1975, the Philadelphia Flyers in 2010, and the Los Angeles Kings in 2015.

95. Hal Winkler got his name engraved on the Stanley Cup when the Boston Bruins won in 1929, but he didn't play with them that season. He had played for Boston the year before but was in the minor leagues during the 1928-29 season. He was credited as the "sub-goaltender."

96. In the early days of the Stanley Cup, the losing team from the finals could challenge the winning team to a rematch, and whoever won would keep the cup.

97. The Toronto Maple Leafs made history during the 1942 Stanley Cup Finals, when they made a comeback after losing the first three games. No other team has accomplished this feat in the finals.

98. The longest game played in the Stanley Cup Finals occurred between the Edmonton Oilers and Boston Bruins in 1990. They played until Petr Kilma of the Oilers scored 15:13 minutes into the third overtime period.

99. The longest game played in the Stanley Cup Finals occurred between the Edmonton Oilers and Boston Bruins in 1990. They played until Petr Kilma of the Oilers scored 15:13 minutes into the third overtime period.

100. The first Stanley Cup was first awarded in 1893 to the Montreal Hockey Club.

101. The original Stanley Cup was seven inches tall, while the current trophy is over three feet tall.

102. There is a person whose job is to keep the Stanley Cup safe. They always travel with the trophy to ensure it isn't harmed. Their official title is "Keeper of the Cup."

103. Lord Stanley of Preston, the Governor General of Canada from 1888 to 1893, donated the Stanley Cup trophy named after him.

104. Jean Beliveau has his name on the Stanley Cup more times than anyone. He won it ten times while playing for the Montreal Canadiens and seven times while working in their office.

105. Eleven NHL teams have never been to the Stanley Cup championships, and 12 have never won.

106. Each band on the Stanley Cup can hold 13 years' worth of team and player names.

107. In the same year the Anaheim Ducks won the Stanley Cup in 2007, they were the league leaders in penalty minutes. The following year, the Detroit Red Wings, with the fewest penalty minutes, won the Stanley Cup.

THE RULEBOOK

Hockey rules and penalties, NHL
standards, and how the game is played.

108. NHL stands for the National Hockey League.

109. Initially, the first rule in the NHL rulebook
was that every game is played on an ice field
called a rink. Now, the first rule specifies the
size of the rink.

110. In the NHL, each hockey puck has the home
team logo on it.

111. While women's ice hockey is played identically
to men's, body checking is not allowed in
women's ice hockey, meaning that fights and
physical contact are not a part of the game as
with men's ice hockey.

112. A goaltender never goes in the penalty box.
If a penalty is given to a goaltender, another
one of his teammates on the ice during the
penalty serves the time for him.

113. A player who commits a game misconduct will be thrown out of the game. This can be for throwing objects from the bench, leaving the penalty box early, or being too aggressive.

114. A minor penalty gives a player two minutes in the box. Examples are interfering with the goaltender and tripping someone.

115. A major penalty earns a player five minutes off the ice, and they'll get one if they're overly violent toward another player.

116. Players who commit three game misconducts in a single season are automatically banned from one match.

117. A misconduct penalty gets players 10 minutes in the box for being unsportsmanlike and/or rude to the officials. Minor penalties are often stacked on top of this.

118. A breakaway describes when the player with the puck has no defending players except for the goaltender between them and the net.

119. No one but the goaltender can touch the puck during the game. If a player happens to have the puck in their hand, they must immediately drop it.

120. "High stick" is when a player raises their stick above the goal post's crossbar or hits another player anywhere above the shoulders with the stick.

121. A player is given a penalty shot if they are interfered with on a breakaway scoring opportunity.

122. There are six different kinds of penalties: minor penalty, major penalty, bench minor penalty, misconduct penalty, match penalty, and penalty shot.

123. A "too many players on the ice" penalty is called when a player entering the game hits the puck or makes contact with an opposing player before the player on their team leaving the game has left the ice.

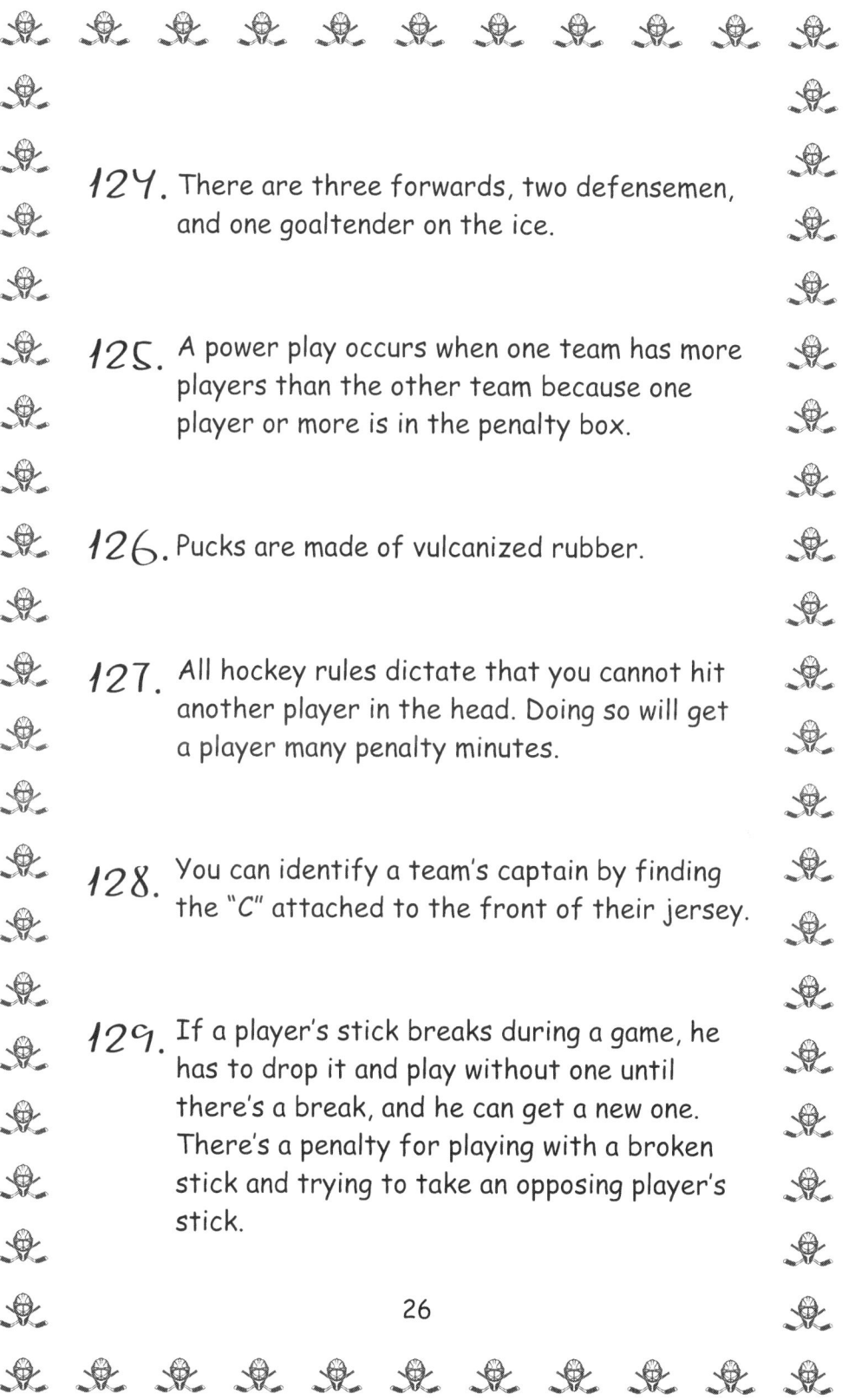

124. There are three forwards, two defensemen, and one goaltender on the ice.

125. A power play occurs when one team has more players than the other team because one player or more is in the penalty box.

126. Pucks are made of vulcanized rubber.

127. All hockey rules dictate that you cannot hit another player in the head. Doing so will get a player many penalty minutes.

128. You can identify a team's captain by finding the "C" attached to the front of their jersey.

129. If a player's stick breaks during a game, he has to drop it and play without one until there's a break, and he can get a new one. There's a penalty for playing with a broken stick and trying to take an opposing player's stick.

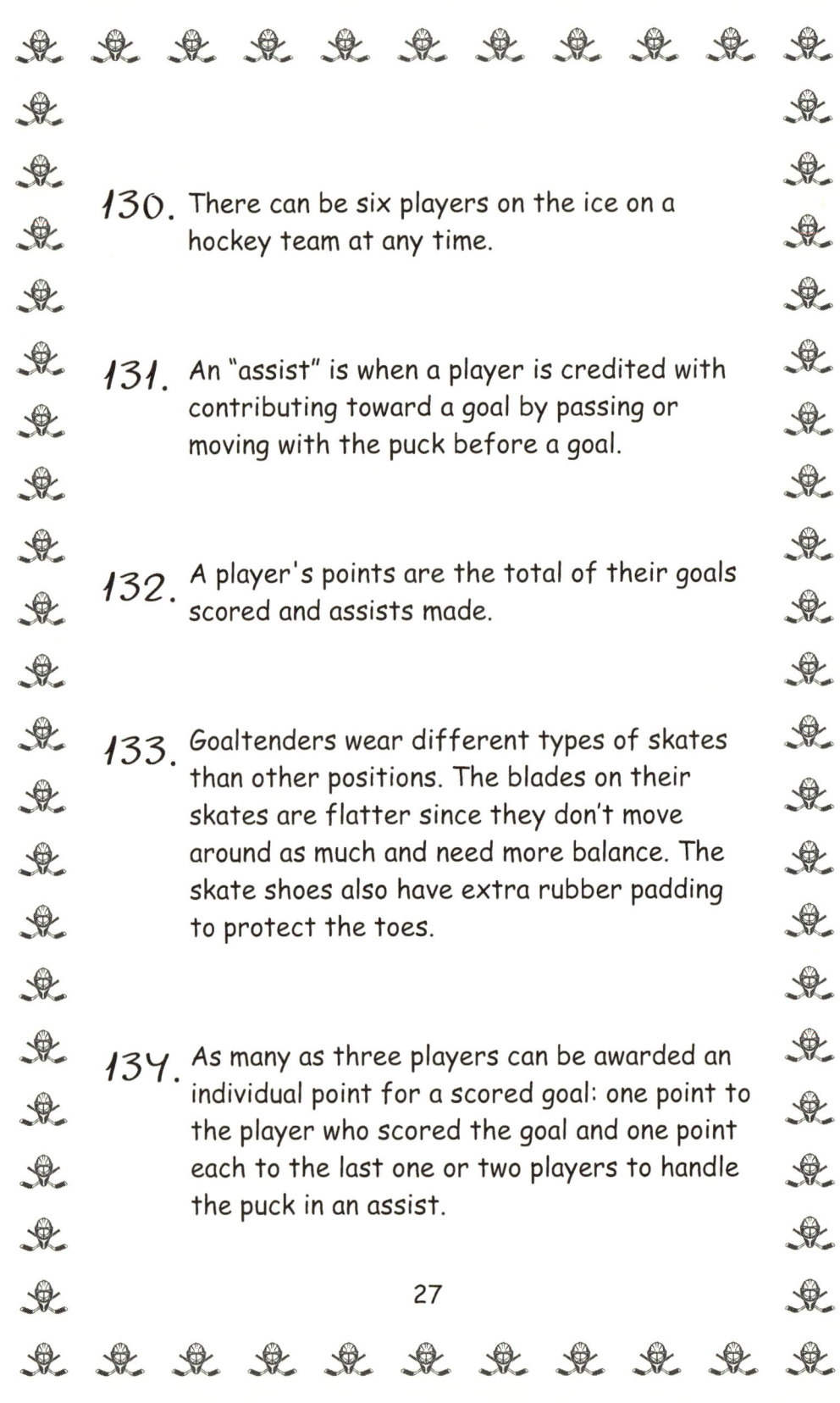

130. There can be six players on the ice on a hockey team at any time.

131. An "assist" is when a player is credited with contributing toward a goal by passing or moving with the puck before a goal.

132. A player's points are the total of their goals scored and assists made.

133. Goaltenders wear different types of skates than other positions. The blades on their skates are flatter since they don't move around as much and need more balance. The skate shoes also have extra rubber padding to protect the toes.

134. As many as three players can be awarded an individual point for a scored goal: one point to the player who scored the goal and one point each to the last one or two players to handle the puck in an assist.

135. A hockey puck is three inches across.

136. Goaltenders' masks are specially designed and usually made to fit the shape and lines of the player's face.

137. A goaltender's full ensemble of equipment weighs about 40 pounds.

138. Ice hockey is the only major sport where substitutions are allowed while the game is in play.

139. There are three popular shots in hockey: slap shot, backhander, and wrist shot.

140. Teams can take their goaltender out of the game and add an extra offense or defense player on the ice instead. This is a risky strategy, as it leaves the net unguarded.

141. An ice hockey goal net is four feet high and six feet wide.

142. NHL games, and most international games, are watched by two referees, two linesmen, and multiple off-ice officials.

143. According to IIHF and NHL rules, the captain and alternate captain are the only players allowed to talk to the referee on the ice during a game. However, many other players do this anyway.

144. According to NHL rules, a goaltender cannot be team captain. However, the Vancouver Canucks made Roberto Luongo their captain anyway for the 2008-09 season, and he wasn't allowed to wear the captain's "C" on his uniform.

145. A hockey puck weighs about six ounces.

146. The machines that resurface the ice rinks during games are called Zambonis. They're named after their creator, Frank J. Zamboni, who developed the first Zamboni in 1949.

147. The home team chooses whether to shoot first or second during a shootout.

148. If a team scores a goal during a power play, the opposite team's player who's in the penalty box returns to the ice, even if their penalty time isn't up yet.

149. Before the beginning of the 1965-66 season, the NHL ruled that every team had to have two dressed goaltenders: one starter and one backup.

150. An NHL ice hockey rink is 200 feet long and 85 feet wide.

151. There are over 70 different penalties in hockey.

152. A hat trick is when a single hockey player scores three goals in a game. The term was first used in the 1800s when fans would throw their hats onto the ice to celebrate the achievement, and the tradition continues today.

153. A shutout is when a goaltender doesn't let the opposing team score any goals during a game.

154. There are 11 players on a hockey team, but only six on the ice at a time.

155. The ice in a professional hockey rink is only about one inch thick. This allows the ice to freeze harder and faster.

156. Before an NHL game, the puck is frozen, so it doesn't bounce.

157. Hockey players play in "shifts" and are only on the ice for about 45 seconds before being swapped out.

158. An NHL hockey puck is one inch thick.

WHERE'S STANLEY NOW?

The Stanley Cup has been to some strange places and done some strange things; here are just a few.

159. Chris Osgood of the Detroit Red Wings took the Stanley Cup to a movie premiere and ate popcorn from it.

160. On his day with the Stanley Cup, Brad Stuart of the Detroit Red Wings had a Stanley Cup-shaped cake made. His stepdaughter ate her piece of cake out of the real Stanley Cup.

161. Luc Robitaille won the Stanley Cup with the Detroit Red Wings in 2002, but since he had played so long with the Los Angeles Kings beforehand, he decided to spend his day with the Stanley Cup, taking it on a tour of Los Angeles.

162. After the Tampa Bay Lightning won the Stanley Cup in 2004, they took the cup to Walt Disney World, where it was marched through the theme park in a parade.

163. Bryan Bickell of the Chicago Blackhawks took the Stanley Cup fishing and put his girlfriend's freshly caught bass in the bowl.

164. The Chicago Blackhawks players took the Stanley Cup to Slovakia in the summer of 2010. One player ate pierogi out of it, while another used it to hold soup.

165. When the New York Islanders won the Stanley Cup in 1980 after many years of losing in the playoffs, player Bryan Trottier took the Stanley Cup home and slept beside it.

166. When Montreal Canadiens coach Scotty Bowman's son was born a few weeks after he won his first Stanley Cup, he named his son Stanley. Stanley ("Stan") Bowman later had his name engraved on the Stanley Cup in 2010 as manager of the Chicago Blackhawks.

167. When Doug Weight won the Stanley Cup with the Carolina Hurricanes in 2006, his wife and three kids ate a massive ice cream sundae from the bowl.

168. Several babies have been placed in the Stanley Cup bowl, but the first known one is Joseph Louis Marcel Vezina, born the day after the Montreal Canadiens won their first Stanley Cup in 1916.

169. A popular legend says the Ottawa Silver Seven players, who won the Stanley Cup in 1905, tried to kick the cup across the Rideau Canal. It didn't make it across but landed on the frozen canal, and they had to wait until the next day to rescue the cup.

170. After the Detroit Red Wings won the Stanley Cup in 2008, player Kris Draper put his newborn daughter in the cup, and she pooped in it.

171. Jean-Sebastien Giguere of the Anaheim Ducks let his dog Henri eat his food from the Stanley Cup bowl.

172. After the New York Rangers won the Stanley Cup in 1994, they returned it in four pieces at the end of the summer. It took 36 hours to put it back together.

173. Following the Montreal Canadiens' Stanley Cup win in 1924, a carload of players took the cup to team owner Leo Dandurand's house for a party. They got a flat tire on the way and put the Stanley Cup outside while replacing it. They realized they had left the Stanley Cup on the road when they got to the party.

174. The Boston Bruins' Adam McQuaid returned home to Prince Edward Island for his day with the Stanley Cup, and he filled the cup with potatoes.

175. Alex Martinez of the Los Angeles Kings scored the winning goal for the Stanley Cup in 2014. On his day with the cup, he ate Fruit Loops out of the bowl.

176. In 2004, the Stanley Cup was supposed to take a flight from Toronto to northern British Columbia, but the plane was full, so the heavy cup was removed. The Hockey Hall of Fame employee traveling with it wasn't told, and he was horrified when the cup didn't appear in the luggage the following day.

177. The Stanley Cup was used in 2014 for the ALS ice bucket charity challenge by Kyle Clifford of the Los Angeles Kings. He filled the cup with ice water and dumped it on his friend.

178. The Stanley Cup was taken to the Native Hockey Tournament in Rankin Inlet, Nunavut, in 2000, where it was -85 degrees Fahrenheit.

179. Cristobal Huet, the third French NHL player in history, took the Stanley Cup to France after the Chicago Blackhawks won it in the 2009-10 season.

180. The captain of the Boston Bruins, Zdeno Chara, took the Stanley Cup to his hometown of Trencin, Slovakia, after the Bruins won the championship in 2011. He brought it to an ancient castle and got to fire a cannon in a special ceremony.

181. When Carolina Hurricanes center Eric Staal brought the Stanley Cup home in 2006, his three younger brothers were scared to touch it because they didn't want to jinx their chances of winning. Later, one of them did: Jordan Staal with the Pittsburgh Penguins in 2009.

182. Maurice "Rocket" Richard chipped two teeth while trying to drink from the Stanley Cup after the Montreal Canadiens won it in 1957.

183. Sylvian Lefebvre got creative with how he used his day with the cup. After winning the cup with the Colorado Avalanches in 1996, he had his daughter baptized in it.

184. The Stanley Cup has appeared in several TV shows.

185. The Toronto Maple Leafs once accidentally used the Stanley Cup as wood for a bonfire, damaging it significantly.

186. The Stanley Cup has ridden on a rollercoaster at Universal Studios Hollywood.

187. The New York Rangers accidentally lit the Stanley Cup on fire while trying to burn something inside it in 1941.

188. Mark Waggoner, who worked for the Colorado Avalanches when they won the Stanley Cup in 2001, took the cup to the top of Mount Elbert, over 14,000 feet tall.

189. After the Pittsburgh Penguins won the Stanley Cup in 2009, Sidney Crosby took it on a jet ski wearing a life jacket.

IMPRESSIVE NUMBERS

The numbers tell the story of some of the most wins, seasons, records, and wackiest situations in NHL history.

190. Bill Reay, coach of the Toronto Maple Leafs, was fired in 1958 following two bad seasons. He moved to the Chicago Blackhawks and became one of the winningest coaches in NHL history, having won over 500 games.

191. Goaltender Gerry Cheevers painted a stitch on his mask every time he got hit in the face. By the end of his career, his mask was nothing but stitches.

192. Goaltender Stephane Beauregard was traded three times in the same off-season. The Winnipeg Jets traded him to the Buffalo Sabres for Christian Ruuttu, the Sabres traded him to the Chicago Blackhawks for Dominik Hasek, and then the Blackhawks traded him back to the Jets for Christian Ruuttu.

193. Grace and Louis Sutter of Alberta, Canada, had seven sons, six of whom played in the NHL: Brian, Darryl, Rich, Duane, Brent, and Ron.

194. Frank Boucher won the Lady Byng Memorial Trophy so many times (seven) that the NHL let him keep it.

195. Francis Clancy is the only NHL player to play all six positions in a single Stanley Cup game, which he did in 1923.

196. Gordie Howe won the Hart Memorial Trophy six times throughout his career.

197. Goaltender Glenn Hall led the NHL in games played for seven years from 1955-1962. He played 70 games each year.

198. Bobby Hull scored over 600 goals while playing for one team, the Chicago Blackhawks.

199. In the fourth game of the Stanley Cup Finals between the Colorado Avalanches and the Florida Panthers, Avalanche goaltender Patrick Roy stopped 63 shots to achieve a shutout in a game that went into triple overtime, winning the cup for the Avalanches.

200. In 1958, five-foot-seven player Henri Richard of the Montreal Canadiens fought three different Boston Bruins players during the same game.

201. Wayne Gretzky won the Art Ross Trophy as the lead scorer in the league ten times throughout his career.

202. Gordie Howe finished in the top ten NHL scorers for 21 straight seasons.

203. The Pittsburgh Penguins played more playoff games than any other team in the 1990s.

204. Montreal Canadiens player Dickie Moore won the Stanley Cup six times, and his name is written on it in five different ways.

205. Lanny McDonald is the only NHL player to score exactly 500 goals in their career.

206. Brothers Maurice and Henri Richard played for the Montreal Canadiens when they won the Stanley Cup five years in a row. They were Maurice's last five years and Henri's first five.

207. It took Raymond Bourque 1826 games to win the Stanley Cup, longer than any other player, and he won it in the last game he played.

208. Wayne Gretzky played in 49 different arenas throughout his career and scored a point in every arena but one.

209. Kristian Huselius scored a goal on his first shot during the first game of the season three times in a row, from the 2001-02 season to the 2005-06 season. The first time it was his first-ever NHL game.

210. Calgary Flames right wing Lanny McDonald won the Stanley Cup for the first time in his last game in 1989. He also scored his 500th goal and made his 1000th point in the same season.

211. After the lockout during the 2004-05 season, over 200 NHL players changed teams.

212. Montreal Canadiens goaltender Ken Dryden won the Stanley Cup six times and the Vezina Trophy five times in his eight seasons, making him one of the best goaltenders in NHL history.

213. Gordie Howe played pro hockey for six decades, from the 1940s to the 1990s.

214. When Mats Sundin beat the Maple Leafs scoring and points record, he was named all of the game's three stars.

THE WOMEN OF HOCKEY

The women who proved it's not just a man's sport.

215. Women started skating in men's hockey games in the 1880s.

216. Finnish hockey player Hayley Wickenheiser became the first woman to score a goal in a men's pro hockey league on February 1, 2003, when she scored one goal and one assist for the Kirkkonummi Lightning.

217. Marguerite Norris became the first female NHL president in the league's history when she became the president of the Detroit Red Wings in 1954.

218. Hayley Wickenheiser was the lead point scorer in women's hockey at the 2002 and 2006 Olympics.

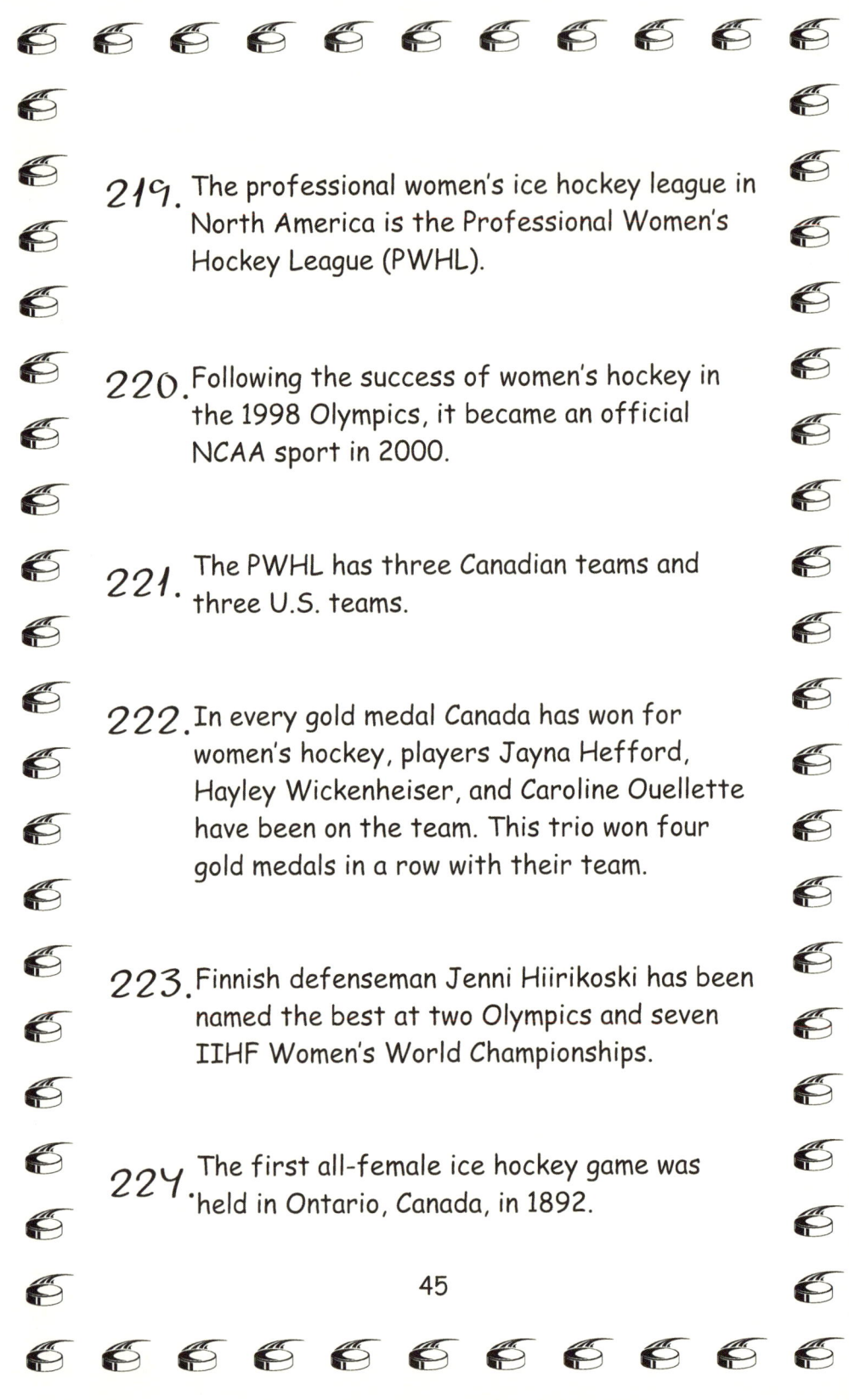

219. The professional women's ice hockey league in North America is the Professional Women's Hockey League (PWHL).

220. Following the success of women's hockey in the 1998 Olympics, it became an official NCAA sport in 2000.

221. The PWHL has three Canadian teams and three U.S. teams.

222. In every gold medal Canada has won for women's hockey, players Jayna Hefford, Hayley Wickenheiser, and Caroline Ouellette have been on the team. This trio won four gold medals in a row with their team.

223. Finnish defenseman Jenni Hiirikoski has been named the best at two Olympics and seven IIHF Women's World Championships.

224. The first all-female ice hockey game was held in Ontario, Canada, in 1892.

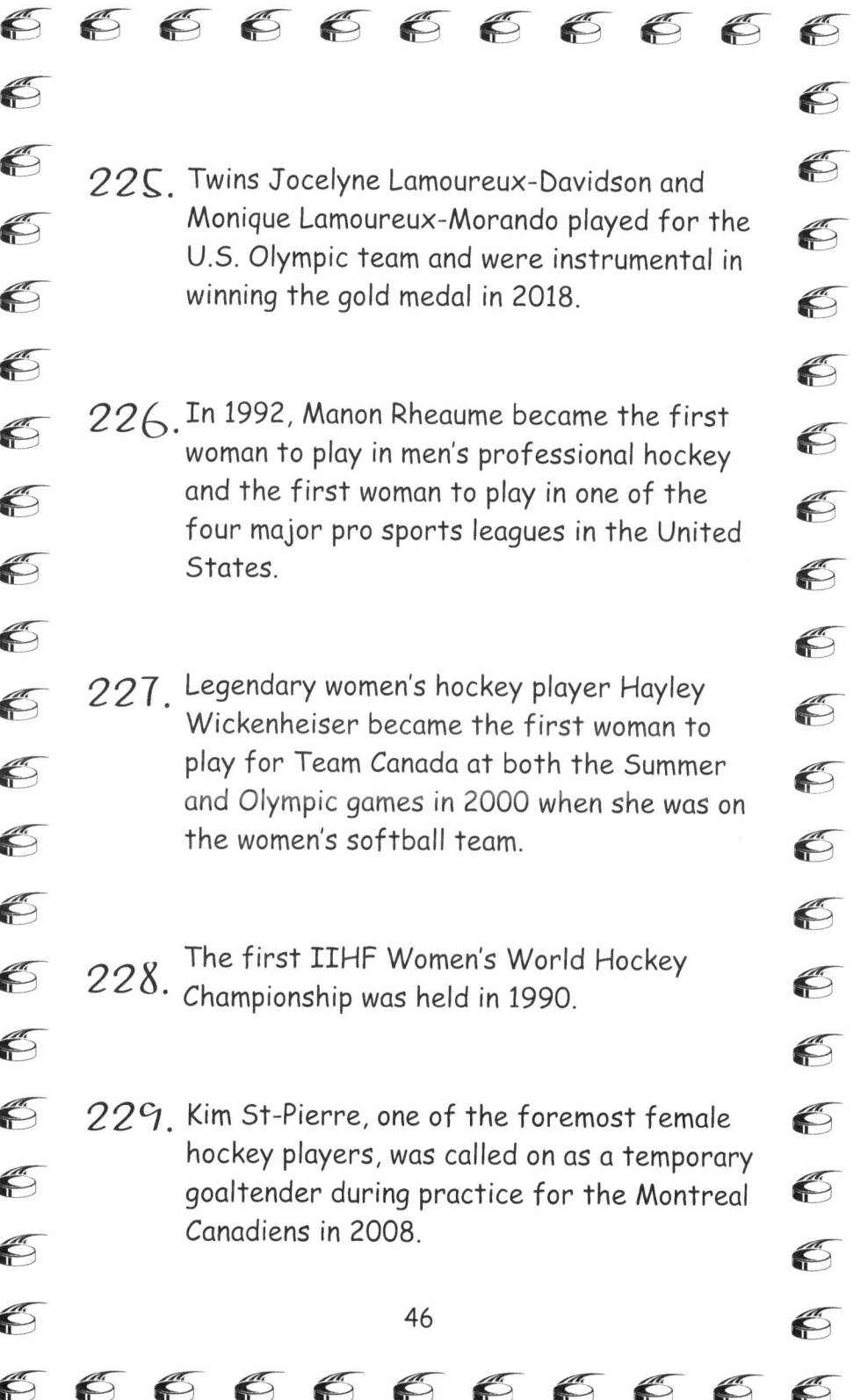

225. Twins Jocelyne Lamoureux-Davidson and Monique Lamoureux-Morando played for the U.S. Olympic team and were instrumental in winning the gold medal in 2018.

226. In 1992, Manon Rheaume became the first woman to play in men's professional hockey and the first woman to play in one of the four major pro sports leagues in the United States.

227. Legendary women's hockey player Hayley Wickenheiser became the first woman to play for Team Canada at both the Summer and Olympic games in 2000 when she was on the women's softball team.

228. The first IIHF Women's World Hockey Championship was held in 1990.

229. Kim St-Pierre, one of the foremost female hockey players, was called on as a temporary goaltender during practice for the Montreal Canadiens in 2008.

46

230. Angela James, Geraldine Heaney, and Cammi Granato were inducted into the IIHF Hall of Fame in 2008, the first time women had been inducted.

231. Hayley Wickenheiser was the first hockey player to be named Canada's female athlete of the year in 2007.

232. Female hockey star Gillian Apps is part of a hockey family. Her grandfather, Syl Apps, played for the Toronto Maple Leafs and is in the Hockey Hall of Fame. Her father, Syl Apps Jr., played with the Pittsburgh Penguins.

233. Marguerite Norris, once president of the Detroit Red Wings, was the first woman to have her name on the Stanley Cup when the team won the championship in 1954 and 1955.

234. Manon Rheaume was the first woman to play in an NHL exhibition game.

235. Angela James and Cammi Granato were the first female inductees into the Hockey Hall of Fame in 2010.

236. The first documented women's ice hockey championship was the Alberta Provincial Women's Championship at the Banff Winter Carnival in 1906.

237. Cassie Campbell was the first women's hockey player in Canada's Sports Hall of Fame.

THEY'RE CALLED WHAT?

Ice hockey has many nicknames—these
are some of the best.

238. Goaltender Frank Brismek earned the nickname "Mr. Zero" after he recorded shutouts in six of his first eight pro games. He ended up with 42 shutouts over his career.

239. Stan Mikita was nicknamed "Mouse" because fans would spell out "Mikita Mouse," a parody of "Mickey Mouse," after he scored a goal.

240. The title of "The Great One" goes to Wayne Gretzky, who is considered the best NHL player in history. He set multiple records, the most prestigious of which is the most career points of all time.

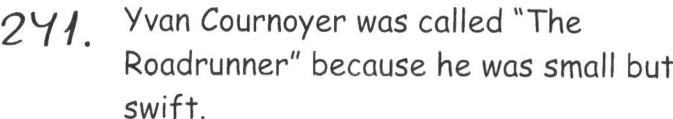

241. Yvan Cournoyer was called "The Roadrunner" because he was small but swift.

242. Igor Larionov of the Detroit Red Wings is nicknamed "the Professor."

243. In the 1970s, the Philadelphia Flyers were nicknamed the "Broad Street Bullies" for their overly aggressive playing style.

244. Mario Lemieux was nicknamed "Super Mario" because he debuted in the NHL the same year the brand-new Super Mario game was released. He was also the third rookie to reach 100 points in a season.

245. Due to the impact he made on the game of hockey, Gordie Howe was given the nickname "Mr. Hockey."

246. As a parody of "The Great One," Wayne Gretzky's brother Brent, who didn't play long for the NHL, is called "The Other One."

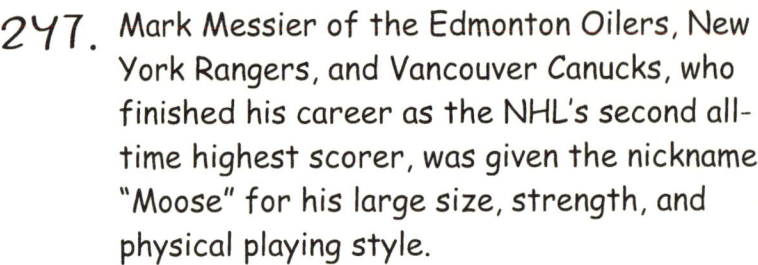

247. Mark Messier of the Edmonton Oilers, New York Rangers, and Vancouver Canucks, who finished his career as the NHL's second all-time highest scorer, was given the nickname "Moose" for his large size, strength, and physical playing style.

248. Known for breaking several records at a young age, including being the youngest NHL captain and the youngest player to get 100 points in a season, Sid "The Kid" Crosby earned his nickname for obvious reasons.

249. Dominik Hasek was called "The Dominator" as a play on his name, and his unique blocking style caused him to dominate games.

250. Dave "The Hammer" Shultz, a member of the Philadelphia Flyers "Broad Street Bullies," was famous for throwing hard punches and being one of the toughest guys on the team, which won the Flyers lots of games, including two Stanley Cups.

251. Bobby Hull's incredible speed earned him the name "The Golden Jet."

252. Noel Acciari of the Florida Panthers was nicknamed "Cookie" by his teammates. Before his first game with the Panthers, he was upset that the pregame meal didn't include cookies, as eating them was part of his routine.

253. Pavel Bure was known as "The Russian Rocket" for being one of the NHL's top scorers in the 1990s.

254. Maurice "The Rocket" Richard got his nickname when one of his teammates mentioned that he looked like a rocket when he skated. A sportswriter heard the story and coined the name, and it became famous.

255. Bernie Geoffrion of the Montreal Canadiens got the strange but powerful nickname "Boom Boom" from being one of the pioneers of the slapshot. There was one boom when he hit the puck, then another when the puck hit the boards. His powerful style brought the Canadiens lots of success in the 1950s.

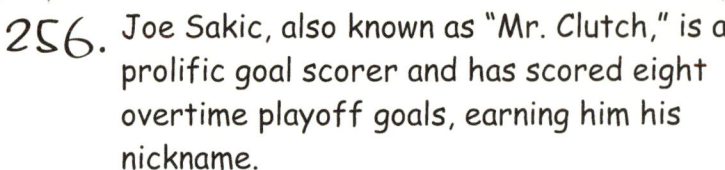

256. Joe Sakic, also known as "Mr. Clutch," is a prolific goal scorer and has scored eight overtime playoff goals, earning him his nickname.

257. Peter "The Great" Forsberg only played 708 games, but he made a massive impact on hockey. He always gave his all out on the ice.

258. Dustin Penner earned his nickname "Penncakes" in an embarrassing way that has nothing to do with hockey. He was about to dive into a stack of pancakes and threw out his back, forcing him to go to the doctor before he could keep playing.

259. Georges Vezina was a goaltender for the Montreal Canadiens in its early days. Not only did he get the best goaltender trophy named after him, but he also got the nickname "The Chicoutimi Cucumber" from the town where he lived and the fact that people said during games he was "cool as a cucumber."

260. Derek Boogaard's name earned him the nickname "The Boogie Man" from teammates and fans because of his large size and stature, which instilled fear in other players.

261. Dave "Tiger" Williams got his nickname from being known as an extremely tough player on the ice.

262. Teemu Selanne was known as the "Finnish Flash," a quick and powerful offensive player who played for the Winnipeg Jets and the Anaheim Ducks and became the highest-scoring Finnish hockey player in the NHL.

263. Dave Semenko got his nickname "Cementhead" from his last name and the fact that he was known to protect Wayne Gretzky while on the ice.

264. Goaltender "Saint" Patrick Roy got his nickname from his role in the Montreal Canadiens' twice Stanley Cup wins.

265. High-scoring player Guy Lefleur was known as "The Flower," the English translation of his last name.

266. Joe Malone was known as "Phantom Joe" because he could handle the puck and move on the ice well. It seemed like he could disappear and reappear at will.

267. Center player Kris Draper earned the nickname "One Dollar Man" when he was traded from the Winnipeg Jets to the Detroit Red Wings for just one dollar in 1993.

268. Glenn Hall, one of the best goaltenders in hockey history, is known as "Mr. Goalie." He played in 502 consecutive games and was instrumental in his teams' success.

269. Rivals Alex Ovechkin and Sidney Crosby achieved hat tricks in the same game on May 4, 2009. The game soon became known as "Dueling Hat Tricks."

HOCKEY'S GREATEST RECORDS

Some of the most memorable ice hockey records have been made and broken.

270. Randy Holt of the Los Angeles Kings holds the record for the most penalty minutes in a single game. He racked up 67 penalty minutes while playing against the Philadelphia Flyers in 1979—that's longer than the 60-minute game itself.

271. In 2023, the Boston Bruins broke the record for most wins during the regular season with 65 victories.

272. Dany Heatley took Wayne Gretzky's record as the youngest All-Star to score a hat trick in 2003; he was one day younger than Wayne.

273. Forty amateur players from Alberta, Canada, set the record for the world's longest hockey game, which lasted 80 hours over four days in 2003.

274. Ray Bourque of the Boston Bruins holds the record for the most shots made at a goal in a single game. He made 19 shots, and the Bruins tied the Quebec Nordiques 3-3 in 1991.

275. Jeff Reese of the Calgary Flames holds the goaltender record for most points scored in a single game (3). They were all assists, meaning he also broke the goaltender record for most assists in a game.

276. Several NHL players are tied for the record of most goals in one period, which is four.

277. Jonathan Huberdeau set the record for most assists by a left-wing player in a single season with 85 assists in the 2021-22 season.

278. The Boston Bruins made the Stanley Cup playoffs for 29 consecutive seasons, from 1967-68 to 1995-96—an NHL record.

279. Jimmy Carson and Bob Kudelski hold the record for the most NHL games played during a regular season. They played 86 games in an 84-game season, Jimmy in 1992-93 and Bob in 1993-94.

280. Ray Bourque has played in the playoffs more years than any other NHL player: 21.

281. Columbus Blue Jackets goaltender Joonas Korpisalo holds the record for most saves in a playoff game. In 2020, he recorded 85 saves against the Tampa Bay Lightning.

282. Jean-Sebastian Giguere holds the record for most overtime hockey played without letting in a goal: 197 minutes and 52 seconds. That's the equivalent of about three full hockey games.

283. Glen Call holds the record for the most consecutive games played by a goaltender, which is 502.

284. Gordie Howe holds the record for most seasons with 20 or more goals: 22.

285. On March 4, 1941, Sam LoPresti made history when he stopped 80 out of 83 goals that were shot at him during a regular season game. This accomplished two records: most shots made and most shots stopped in a regular season game.

286. Dale Hawerchuck holds the record for being the youngest 100-point player. He was only 18 when he accomplished this with the Winnipeg Jets.

287. Johnny Bower is the oldest player to win the Stanley Cup. He was 42 when the Toronto Maple Leafs won in 1967.

288. Bobby Orr and Phil Esposito of the Boston Bruins hold the record for being the first teammates to lead the NHL in scoring in the first and second spots five years in a row, 1969-1975.

289. Wayne and Brent Gretzky hold the record for most combined points by two brothers in the NHL.

290. The Detroit Red Wings hold the NHL record for most wins in a season when they won 62 games in the 1995-96 season.

291. The Montreal Canadiens have retired 15 jerseys, more than any other team.

292. Martin Brodeur holds the record for most career victories, 691, all but three with the New Jersey Devils.

293. Only two coaches have won the Stanley Cup with more than one team: Tommy Gorman and Scott Bowman, who coached several teams.

294. Dominik Hasek of the Buffalo Sabres, Detroit Red Wings, and other teams holds the record for highest goaltender save percentage at .922.

295. Chris Chelios has played in 266 playoff games, the most out of any NHL player.

296. Pavel Bure of the Florida Panthers and Valeri Bure of the Calgary Flames hold the record for the highest combined goals between two brothers in a single season. They achieved this in the 1999-2000 season with 93 goals.

297. Wayne Gretzky and Brett Hull hold the record for most game-winning goals scored in the Stanley Cup playoffs, which is 24.

298. Larry Hillman was the youngest player on a team to ever win the Stanley Cup at 18 years old in 1955.

299. Sidney Crosby, who was 21 years old when the Pittsburgh Penguins won the Stanley Cup, was the youngest person to captain a team to the championship.

300. Steve Yzerman was the youngest captain the Detroit Red Wings ever had and the longest-serving captain in history after he led his team for 20 seasons.

301. The record for the two fastest goals scored in a game goes to Nels Stewart of the Montreal Maroons and Deron Quint of the Winnipeg Jets. They both scored two goals within four seconds of each other.

302. Joe Malone holds the record for scoring average per game, 2.2 goals. A player must score 180 goals in 82 games to beat the record.

303. Mike Sillinger has played for more teams than any other NHL player. He played for 12 different teams during his career.

304. Gordie Howe had the longest pro hockey career at 32 years. He began playing with the Detroit Red Wings in 1946 and retired after the 1979-80 season.

305. Brian Boucher of the Phoenix Coyotes was most often a backup goaltender, but during a brief time as a starter during the 2003-04 season, he recorded five shutouts in a row, a modern pro hockey record.

306. Patrick Roy is the only NHL player to have won the Conn Smythe Trophy three times.

307. Bill Mosienko of the Chicago Blackhawks scored the fastest hat trick in NHL history in 21 seconds.

308. On February 10, 2007, Jordan Staal became the youngest NHL player to score a hat trick at 18.

309. The Buffalo Sabres hold the record for most goals in a single period with nine goals against the Toronto Maple Leafs in 1981.

310. Bobby and Dennis Hull have the most combined career goals out of any NHL brothers in history: 913.

311. Robbie Irons had the shortest NHL career in history. He was a backup goaltender who only played for three minutes and one second for the St. Louis Blues during a game in 1968.

312. Armand Guidolin became the youngest player in NHL history when he joined the Boston Bruins at 16 for the 1942-43 season. At the time, there was a shortage of players because of World War II.

313. The Rat Portage Thistles became the team to own the Stanley Cup for the shortest time when the losing Montreal Wanderers challenged them for the cup in 1907 and won.

314. Ken Dryden of the Montreal Canadiens and Dave Dryden of the Buffalo Sabres are the only goaltender brothers to face each other in NHL history.

315. The way Mats Sundin became the top-scoring Toronto Maple Leafs player in 2007 is very interesting. He broke the point record when he was credited with an assist during the game, but he hadn't touched the puck and admitted the fact. The assist was taken away, but later in the game, Mats scored a goal, giving him both the goal and overall points record for the Maple Leafs.

316. John and Charlotte Grahame made history as the only mother-son duo with their names engraved on the Stanley Cup. John played for the Tampa Bay Lightning, who won in 2004, while his mom worked in the Colorado Avalanche's office when they won in 2001.

317. Joe Malone of the Montreal Canadiens scored eight goals in a game in 1920, setting the record for most goals made by one player in a single game.

318. Zdeno Chara of the Boston Bruins made the fastest-recorded shot in NHL history in 2012. He shot the puck at 108.8 miles per hour.

319. The longest NHL game in history was between the Detroit Red Wings and Montreal Maroons in 1936. The match lasted over six hours, with about 176 minutes of playtime. Ultimately, the Red Wings won 1-0 after 116 minutes and 30 seconds of overtime.

320. The smallest draft in NHL history took place in 1965, when only 11 players were selected.

321. Wayne Gretzky holds 61 NHL records.

322. The Montreal Canadiens have won more Stanley Cup championships than any other NHL team (24).

323. Bobby Orr, who scored 139 points in the 1970-71 season, holds the record for most points by a defenseman in a season.

324. Henri Richards of the Montreal Canadiens has won more Stanley Cups than any NHL player (11).

325. Forward player Tiger Williams holds the record for most career penalty minutes in the NHL: 3,966.

326. NHL coach Scotty Bowman won more Stanley Cups than any other head coach (9).

327. Phil Kessel is called the NHL's "Ironman," as he holds the record for most consecutive games played. He's played over 1000 games in a row as of 2024.

328. Canada has the most players in the Hockey Hall of Fame.

329. At the start of the 2022-23 season, the Boston Bruins broke the NHL record for most home wins in a row at the start of the season (14).

330. On December 10, 2022, Jack Hughes of the New Jersey Devils played the longest shift in NHL history when he was on the ice for six minutes and two seconds straight.

331. Wayne Gretzky holds the record for the longest consecutive point streak, with at least one point earned in 51 games in a row.

332. Sam and Pete LoPresti are the only father and son to both record an NHL shutout.

333. In 2023, the Boston Bruins set a new record for the most points accrued in the regular season (135).

334. Evander Kane of the Edmonton Oilers beat Wayne Gretzky's record of the quickest five hat tricks ever. Wayne did it in 136 games, while Evander did it in 130.

335. The record for most penalty minutes accrued in a single NHL game is 419 in 2004 between the Ottawa Senators and Philadelphia Flyers.

336. The largest NHL draft in history was in 2000, when 293 players were picked.

337. Dave Shultz holds the record for most penalty minutes in a season with 472 minutes in the 1974-75 season.

338. As of 2024, Alexander Ovechkin has scored 843 career goals, putting him in second place just behind Wayne Gretzky.

TRADITIONS AND SUPERSTITIONS

From the cool to the bizarre, here are some of the most interesting traditions and superstitions in ice hockey.

339. Hockey players have many superstitions, or things they always do before games because they believe it helps their chances of winning.

340. The Florida Panthers have a strange tradition where their fans throw fake rats onto the ice after their team scores a goal. This all began when Panthers captain Scott Mellanby found a rat in the locker room and hit it with his hockey stick, going on to score two goals during the game in 1995.

341. The Winnipeg Jets created the now-famous playoff tradition of the "White Out," where fans wear white. It was on April 10, 1985, in a game against the Calgary Flames.

342. Petr Kilma of the Detroit Red Wings broke his stick each time he scored a goal because he believed a stick would only work well for one goal. Throughout his career, he made 408 goals—and supposedly broke 408 sticks.

343. Georges Laraque of the Pittsburgh Penguins often celebrates scoring a goal by smashing himself into the glass on the rink's edge.

344. Many hockey players believe that not shaving during the playoffs will give them a better chance of winning. During the playoffs, there's lots of long hair on the ice!

345. After each NHL game, three players are named "stars of the game," with the first being the best player.

346. Many hockey players believe it's bad luck to touch the Stanley Cup before they've won it.

347. Between periods, Wayne Gretzky drank several different drinks in a specific order: Diet Coke, water, Gatorade, and a second Diet Coke.

348. Sidney Crosby doesn't talk to his mother before a game because he believes it keeps him from getting hurt.

349. Goaltender Patrick Roy talked to the goalposts to convince them to be on his side during games.

350. Hockey players, coaches, staff, and anyone related to the team know not to step on the team logo in the middle of the locker room. They believe it represents the team and should never be disrespected by being stood on.

351. Wayne Gretzky put baby powder on the end of his hockey stick before every game, a tradition many other players have adopted since then.

352. Many hockey teams have a specific song they listen to right before they get out onto the ice before every game. From pop and country to rock 'n' roll, hockey teams listen to it all.

ONE FOR THE TEAMS

It's all about ice hockey teams: names, places, and everything else.

353. In 1991, because of a disagreement between the Minnesota North Star owners, the team split into two: Minnesota and the San Jose Sharks.

354. The New Jersey Devils were originally the Kansas City Scouts, then the Colorado Rockies, before moving to New Jersey after the 1981-82 season.

355. The Calgary Flames were originally the Atlanta Flames, based in Atlanta, Georgia. In 1981, they moved to Canada.

356. The San Jose Sharks once lost 71 games in a season. Their record in the 1992-93 season was 11-71-2. The following year, however, they made the playoffs.

357. The Montreal Canadiens' official name is le Club de Hockey Canadien, so they have an "H" on their jerseys.

73

358. It took a while for Detroit to land on their team name. The franchise began as the Victoria Cougars, then the Detroit Cougars. They were renamed the Detroit Falcons in 1930, and in 1932, they finally settled on Red Wings.

359. The Philadelphia Flyers were named after the city held a contest to name the team. They received 25,000 entries, and the winning name came from a child.

360. Even though Vancouver is on Canada's west coast, the Vancouver Canucks were put in the NHL East Division in 1970 because the league thought it would be a better balance of original and expansion teams.

361. "Canuck"—like the Vancouver Canucks—is a slang word that just means Canadian.

362. The Tampa Bay Lightning got their name because the city of Tampa is the lightning capital of the United States.

363. The Columbus Blue Jackets chose their name to honor the fact that Ohio contributed more of its population to the Union Army than any other state during the American Civil War. The Union Army wore blue jackets, many made in Columbus.

364. Following the 2004-05 lockout, the San Jose Sharks was the only team not adding a new player to its roster.

365. From 1926 to 1996, the Montreal Canadiens used the Montreal Forum as their home arena, where they won over 1500 games.

366. The Washington Capitals got their name because Washington, D.C. is the capital city of the United States.

367. The Washington Capitals got their name because Washington, D.C. is the capital city of the United States.

368. The Winnipeg Jets became the Arizona Coyotes in 1996.

369. When another team was added to New York for the 1972-73 season, they named themselves the Islanders because the team was based on Long Island.

370. Frederic McLaughlin decided to name his new Chicago team "Blackhawks" in 1926 because he served in what was known as the "Black Hawks Division" in World War I.

371. Since St. Louis, Missouri, is famous for the blues music style, it seemed only fitting that the city's hockey team should be called the "St. Louis Blues."

372. The team name "Bruins" comes from the word "bruin," a name for "bear" used in old stories.

373. The name of the Winnipeg Jets was inspired by the National Football League (NFL) New York Jets team.

374. The oldest pro hockey team in the NHL is the Montreal Canadiens, established in 1909.

375. During a Red Wings playoff game in 1952, two fans threw an octopus onto the ice, representing the eight wins they hoped the team would get to take home the Stanley Cup (as there were only six teams in the NHL at the time). The octopus eventually became the Red Wings' mascot.

HOCKEY HISTORY

A look back at how hockey has evolved
over the years.

376. No one is exactly sure where and when ice hockey originated. Both ice and field hockey have been traced back to ancient civilizations that played similar games. However, it is known for sure that the modern version of ice hockey was developed and made popular in Canada in the 1800s.

377. The first-ever organized ice hockey game was played in 1875 in Montreal, Canada.

378. The first pro ice hockey league was the International Pro Hockey League in Michigan. It started in the 1910-11 season.

379. The NHL was founded in 1917.

380. In the 1980s, hockey pucks were made from recycled tires.

376. No one is exactly sure where and when ice hockey originated. Both ice and field hockey have been traced back to ancient civilizations that played similar games. However, it is known for sure that the modern version of ice hockey was developed and made popular in Canada in the 1800s.

377. The first-ever organized ice hockey game was played in 1875 in Montreal, Canada.

378. The first pro ice hockey league was the International Pro Hockey League in Michigan. It started in the 1910-11 season.

379. The NHL was founded in 1917.

380. In the 1980s, hockey pucks were made from recycled tires.

381. James Creighton is often recognized as the creator of ice hockey. While growing up in Nova Scotia, he played the game and taught it to his new friends in Montreal, which is how the modern version of ice hockey began to spread. He also created the original rules.

382. Before the NHL was formed, it was known as the National Hockey Association (NHA), which began in 1910.

383. In 1967, the NHL expanded from six original teams to 12 teams, one of the largest expansions in pro sports history.

384. When ice hockey first started, a seventh player called a rover played between the offense and defense.

385. The first NHL game with a team composed of all-star players took place in 1934 as a benefit for injured player Ace Bailey.

386. The Stanley Cup finals were first broadcast on TV in 1953, depicting a game between the Montreal Canadiens and Boston Bruins.

387. On May 12, 1994, the Canadian government passed a bill declaring hockey as Canada's winter sport.

388. When NHL games were first broadcast on TV and radio, the broadcasts didn't start until well after the game had already begun. Team owners worried that if people could listen to or watch the whole game for free wherever they were, no one would buy tickets to see the game live.

389. The first official NHL All-Star game was played on October 13, 1947. The Toronto Maple Leafs played against a team of NHL all-stars.

390. In 1984, Canada's first astronaut, Dr. Marc Garneau, carried a puck when he blasted into outer space on the space shuttle Challenger.

391. The 2004-05 NHL season was canceled due to a lockout caused by a disagreement on salary between hockey players and NHL owners.

392. Sled hockey was first developed by three athletes in wheelchairs in 1961 in Stockholm, Sweden.

393. When hockey first started, there were two 30-minute periods instead of three 20-minute periods.

394. The CKCK radio station in Regina, Canada, was the first to broadcast a full professional hockey game on March 14, 1923.

395. The first shootout in the NHL happened on the first day of the 2005-06 season after introducing the shootout rule. It was during a 2-2 game between the Ottawa Senators and Toronto Maple Leafs.

396. Jerry Toppazzini of the Boston Bruins was the last position player to take over as goaltender in 1960.

397. In the 1920s, goaltenders originally wore British cricket pads on their legs. However, pucks sometimes bounced off them and went straight into the net anyway, so wider pads were developed.

398. The current format of the Stanley Cup playoffs—the best of seven games—was introduced in 1939.

399. Emil Kenesky, a leather worker and hockey fan, began developing the standard goaltender leg pads in 1924.

400. When ice hockey was first played, the sticks were made of wood. Today, most sticks are made of carbon fiber.

401. The NHL originally had just six teams, now called the Original Six.

INCREDIBLE ROOKIES

These players did some amazing things
in their first year.

402. Goaltender Tom Barrasso was drafted into the Buffalo Sabres right out of high school and won the Calder Memorial Trophy and Vezina Trophy in his rookie year.

403. Goaltender Ken Dryden is the only NHL rookie to win an individual league trophy before winning the Calder Trophy. He started playing with the Montreal Canadiens late in the season and was so outstanding that he won the Conn Smythe Trophy after the playoffs. He was awarded the Calder Trophy after his first full year in the NHL.

404. Mike Bossy was the first NHL player to score 50 goals in his rookie season.

405. Gus Bodnar scored his first NHL goal just 15 seconds into his very first game with the Toronto Maple Leafs, a record for the fastest career goal that still stands today.

406. Kent Douglas was the first defenseman to win the Calder Memorial Trophy for the best rookie in the 1962-63 season.

407. Teemu Selanne holds the record for most goals scored by a rookie in the NHL (76).

408. Al Hill holds the record for most points by a player in his first NHL game. On February 14, 1977, he racked up five points.

409. When he played his first game for the St. Louis Blues at 38, Connie Madigan was the oldest rookie in NHL history.

410. Connor Bedard of the Chicago Blackhawks holds the record for the youngest player to score a goal within the first 30 seconds of a game. He was 18 years old and in his rookie season.

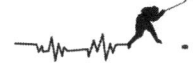

NOTABLE PLAYERS

Interesting facts about fantastic
hockey players.

411. British Olympic hockey player Archibald Stinchcombe was blind in one eye.

412. Dave Shultz of the Philadelphia Flyers spent so much time in the penalty box that he recorded a song called "The Penalty Box.

413. Wayne Gretzky's number 99 jersey was retired across the entire NHL in February 2000.

414. Mario Lemieux's brother, Alain Lemieux, played in the NHL for the St. Louis Blues and Quebec Nordiques. Over 119 games, he racked up 28 goals and 44 assists.

415. Len Ceglarski of the 1952 U.S. Olympic ice hockey team also played baseball.

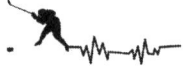

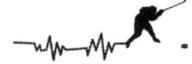

416. Wayne Gretzky's brother Brent also played briefly in the NHL for the Tampa Bay Lightning, and the brothers once faced off against each other.

417. .Wayne Gretzky didn't win the Calder Memorial Trophy for best rookie in his first year in the NHL because he had already played for the World Hockey Association (WHA), which disqualified him from the award. Ray Bourque of the Boston Bruins

418. won the award instead.

The Buffalo Sabres once drafted a player who didn't exist. As a prank, Paul Weiland

419. came up with a fake player named Taro Tsujimoto, whom the Sabres drafted successfully until the NHL president found out and the pick was called invalid.

When Wayne Gretzky was behind the net, fans would say he was "in his office" because he scored so many points from there.

421. Major League Baseball (MLB) pitcher Tom Glavine was drafted by the Los Angeles Kings into the NHL in 1984, but he never played a game.

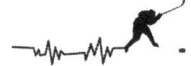

420. After the NHL ruled that teams had to have a backup goaltender, Ross "Lefty" Wilson became the most famous backup. He had been a goaltender in the minor leagues and was an assistant trainer for the Detroit Red Wings. He played 85 minutes between 1953 and 1957 and only let in one goal.

422. Sidney Crosby's number 87 reflected his birthday. He was born on August 7th, 1987.

423. When he started playing hockey, Wayne Gretzky first wore the number 9 on his jersey in honor of Gordie Howe. As he moved up to a different team, number 9 was taken, so he tried a couple of other numbers before deciding on 99.

424. There have only been six players in the NHL to have their jerseys retired by two different teams.

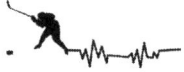

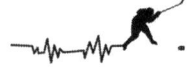

425. In the 1970s, famous players Denis Savard, Denis Cyr, and Denis Tremblay were all on the Montreal Junior Canadiens team and formed a line called "Les Trois Denis" or "The Three Denises." They all shared the same first name, were born on the same day, and lived within three blocks of each other.

426. Before teams were required to have backup goaltenders, if the goaltender got hurt, any player on the ice could replace them. Defenseman Harry Mummery of the Ottawa Senators was the first player to do this.

427. Three goaltenders—Clint Benedict, Frank McCool, and Martin Brodeur — have achieved three shutouts in a Stanley Cup Finals game.

428. Most people know that Gordie Howe played with his sons Mark and Marty, but Gordie's brother Vic also played in the NHL for the New York Rangers.

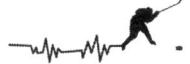

429. In the 1928 Stanley Cup Finals, New York Rangers coach Lester Patrick became famous for stepping in as his team's goaltender when he was hurt. Lester only let in one shot and helped the Rangers clinch the victory.

430. Connie Broden is the only hockey player to win the World Championship and the Stanley Cup in the same season.

431. Brian, Darryl, Duane, and Brent Sutter, four of the six famous Sutter brothers, became NHL coaches.

432. Doug McKay is the only NHL player to play his only NHL game in the Stanley Cup Finals with the team that would win the cup.

433. Bobby Orr is the only defenseman ever to win the Art Ross Trophy.

434. Only one player, Billy Coutu of the Montreal Canadiens and Boston Bruins, has ever received a life suspension from pro hockey for being too aggressive during a game.

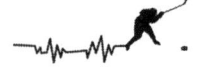

435. Famous Boston Bruins goaltender Tuukka Rask has a species of Kenyan wasp named after him. It's called Thaumatodryinus tuukkaraski.

436. Defenseman Scott Niedermayer is the only player to win all the following awards during his career: the World Junior gold medal, World Hockey League Player of the Year, Canadian Hockey League Player of the Year, NHL All-Star member, Norris Trophy, Stanley Cup, Conn Smythe Trophy, and Olympic Gold medal.

GOING FOR OLYMPIC GOLD

On hockey at the Olympics.

---

437. Ice hockey first appeared in the Olympics at the 1920 Summer Olympics in Antwerp, Belgium. After that, it was moved to the Winter Olympics.

438. Canada won the very first ice hockey Olympic gold medal in 1920. The United States got silver and Czechoslovakia bronze.

439. Buffalo Sabre player Dominik Hasek led the Czech Republic to the ice hockey gold medal in 1998.

440. In 2006, Sweden won both Olympic gold and the IIHF World Championship.

441. In 1998, the first year women's ice hockey was in the Olympics, only six women's hockey teams competed.

442. Gerry Geran was the first former NHL player to compete in the Olympics. He played for the United States team in 1920 and 1924 before returning to the NHL.

443. Jaroslav Drobny, a member of the silver-medal-winning Czechoslovakian Olympic ice hockey team, became a professional tennis player and won a Wimbledon singles title.

444. At the 1960 Olympic Games, the United States won their first gold medal in ice hockey.

445. Australia's first foray into Olympic ice hockey didn't go well. In 1960, they lost all six games they played, scored ten goals, and let their opponents score 88 goals overall.

446. At the 1964 Olympic Games, head coach David Bauer was hit on the head with a broken stick flung by a Swedish player. Team Canada wanted revenge, but David was calm and forgiving. Even though Canada's hockey team came in fourth at the Olympics, David was awarded a gold medal from the IIHF for sportsmanship.

447. Men's ice hockey became an official Olympic sport in 1920.

448. Canada and Sweden boycotted ice hockey at the 1976 Winter Olympics because professional athletes weren't allowed to compete, while countries like the Soviet Union circumvented this rule by having "professional amateurs" on their teams.

449. The final Olympic gold medal game came down to a shootout for the first time in 1994. Sweden and Canada finished regulation time with a score of 2-2, and Sweden won the shootout and the gold.

450. The United States won the first-ever Olympic gold medal for women's hockey in 1998.

451. Jarome Iginla became the first Black male to win a gold medal at the Winter Olympics when he won with Team Canada's ice hockey team in 2002.

452. The first women's Olympic ice hockey game was played in 1998.

453. Canada lost its first hockey gold medal at the 1936 Olympic Games, which it lost to Great Britain—although most British players lived in Canada.

454. The Soviet Union competed in its first Olympics in 1956 and won the gold medal in ice hockey. In all, they totaled more gold medals than any other country.

455. In 1980, the United States ice hockey team pulled off an impossible win against the dominating Soviet Union team at the Olympics, resulting in one of the most famous hockey games in history, "Miracle on Ice."

456. Ice hockey at the Olympics was first open to professionals in 1998.

457. When Canada won the gold medal for hockey at the 2002 Olympics (once NHL players could participate in international competition), it was the first time in 50 years that Canada had won a gold medal.

458. As of 2024, the United States and Canada have competed for women's hockey gold at the Olympics six times.

459. Only six hockey players in history have won the Stanley Cup and an Olympic gold medal in the same season.

460. Sled hockey entered the Paralympic Winter Games in 1994.

461. Ken Morrow was the first hockey player to win an Olympic gold medal and the Stanley Cup in the same year.

462. The Winnipeg Falcons represented Canada at ice hockey's first appearance at the Olympics in 1920.

463. Canada holds the most Olympic gold medals in hockey (14, as of 2024).

464. Harry Watson was one of the foremost players in the first Olympic ice hockey team. He scored 36 goals throughout the tournament, which is still a record for today's Olympics.

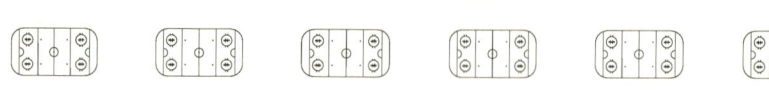

HOCKEY AROUND THE WORLD

A look at ice hockey as an international sport.

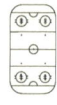

465. Worldwide, there are about 1.6 million registered hockey players, both young and old, and the number of players grows every year.

466. In 1908, the International Ice Hockey Federation (IIHF) was formed in Europe. Belgium, Switzerland, France, Bohemia, and Great Britain were the first five members.

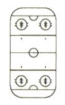

467. More children are registered to play ice hockey in Canada than in any other country.

468. The first international hockey tournament was held in Switzerland in 1910, and Great Britain won.

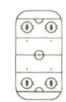

469. The IIHF World Junior Championship began in the 1981-82 season. There were eight teams, and Canada won the 1982 championship.

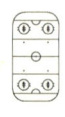

470. Canada has won more World Junior Championships than any other country.

471. The highest-scoring IIHF game occurred between Bulgaria and Slovakia on September 6, 2008, in a women's ice hockey Olympic qualifier game. Slovakia won 82-0.

472. The first international regular-season NHL game was played in Japan between the Vancouver Canucks and Anaheim Ducks in 1997.

473. The International Ice Hockey Federation (IIHF) governs all international ice hockey.

COLLEGE HOCKEY

It isn't just about the NHL! The history of
college ice hockey is just as interesting.

474. The National College Athletic Association
(NCAA) governs college ice hockey and many
other popular sports like American football,
basketball, and soccer.

475. The championship playoff for college hockey
is the NCAA Frozen Four.

476. About one-third of NHL players are involved
in NCAA programs in college before making
it to pro hockey.

477. At the first men's ice hockey Frozen Four in
1948, Michigan won the championship
against Dartmouth.

478. In 1926, the NCAA—which mainly dealt with
American football at the time—started
getting involved in college hockey.

479. The American Women's College Hockey
Alliance (AWCHA) was formed in 1997. It
was around for a few years before the
NCAA decided to govern women's hockey.

480. New Hampshire became the United States'
first national champion in women's college
hockey when it beat Brown in the
championship game in 1998.

481. The Frozen Four wasn't officially named as
such until 1999, although the term started
being used in 1998.

482. The first Women's Frozen Four took place in
2001 when the Minnesota Duluth Bulldogs
won the championship after beating St.
Lawrence University.

483. 2020 was the first time in 72 years a
national college hockey champion wasn't
crowned due to the COVID-19 pandemic.

484. In the men's Frozen Four championship in
2021, three of the four teams competing
were from Minnesota.

FUN FACTS

There's always more to learn about ice hockey; check out these final fun facts!

485. Jerseys are sometimes still called sweaters because players initially wore sweaters to ward off the cold.

486. The Hockey Hall of Fame is in Toronto, Canada. The U.S. Hockey Hall of Fame is located in Eveleth, Minnesota.

487. The commissioner of the NHL is in charge of the entire league. As of 2024, the position has only ever been filled by one person, Gary Bettman, who has filled the role since it was created in 1993.

488. Inglasco in Sherbrooke, Quebec, Canada, makes all of the NHL's pucks.

489. On November 10, 1979, in a game between the Minnesota North Stars and Los Angeles Kings, only one puck was used for the whole game.

490. The longest-running sports show in Canada is Hockey Night in Canada

491. From 2002 to 2013, all five-dollar bills printed in Canada had a picture on the back of children participating in winter activities, including hockey.

492. Wayne Gretzky wanted to be a baseball player when he was a kid.

493. In 2014 the Nashville Predators played an away game against the Toronto Maple Leafs. Before the game, the singer's microphone cut out during "The Star-Spangled Banner," and Toronto fans finished the song for her. A few months later, when the Maple Leafs played in Nashville, Nashville fans thanked them by singing "O Canada."

494. In January 1978, a snowstorm delayed a game between the New Jersey Devils and Calgary Flames for almost two hours. Only 334 fans made it to the game.

495. Only three goaltenders have ever been picked first overall in the NHL draft.

496. Gordie Howe sometimes went to batting practice with the Detroit Tigers while playing for the Detroit Red Wings.

497. There are 32 teams in the NHL as of 2024. Seven of the teams are Canadian, and 25 are American.

498. There are 32 teams in the NHL as of 2024. Seven of the teams are Canadian, and 25 are American.

499. Sled hockey is a way for athletes with physical disabilities to play ice hockey. Players in this sport use special sleds and sticks to get around on the ice.

500. During one game in 2023 between the Florida Panthers and Ottawa Senators, all ten players on the ice got involved in a fight. Since there were only seven minutes left in the game and they all earned 10-minute penalties, they were considered ejected from the game.

501. The 2024 NHL draft will take place in the Vegas Sphere, an 18,600-seat sphere covered in LED lights on the inside. The NHL is the first sports entity to hold an event at this highly-coveted venue.

REFERENCES

If you would like to check the references for the facts, you can do so by scanning this QR code!

Manufactured by Amazon.ca
Bolton, ON

52322906R00062